Las Abuelas
STORIES FROM
OUR KITCHENS

THE HALI'A ALOHA SERIES

Las Abuelas
STORIES FROM OUR KITCHENS

MARIA J. GUTIERREZ

LEGACY ISLE
PUBLISHING

THE HALIʻA ALOHA SERIES
Darien Hsu Gee, Series Editor

Haliʻa Aloha ("cherished memories") by Legacy Isle Publishing is a guided memoir program developed in collaboration with series editor Darien Hsu Gee. The series celebrates moments big and small, harnessing the power of short forms to preserve the lived experiences of the storytellers. To become a Haliʻa Aloha author, please visit www.legacyislepublishing.net.

Legacy Isle Publishing is an imprint of Watermark Publishing, based in Honolulu, Hawaiʻi, and dedicated to "Telling Hawaiʻi's Stories" through memoirs, corporate biographies, family histories and other books.

© 2022 Maria J. Gutierrez

All rights reserved. No part of this book may be reproduced in any form or by any electronic or mechanical means, including information retrieval systems, without prior written permission from the publisher, except for brief passages quoted in reviews.

Names in this book have been changed to protect the privacy of the individuals involved.

ISBN 978-1-948011-89-1 (print)
ISBN 978-1-948011-90-7 (ebook)

Legacy Isle Publishing
1000 Bishop St., Ste. 806
Honolulu, HI 96813
Telephone 1-808-587-7766
Toll-free 1-866-900-BOOK
www.legacyislepublishing.net

Printed in the United States

Dedicated to my daughters, Riley and Mac,
and in loving memory of my mom and grandmothers

CONTENTS

Preface	1
Introduction	2
Matriarchal Ode	4
Ancestors Assemble	5

I. La Cocina

Mother Tree One	8
Christmas Eve Tamales	9
Rolling in the Dough	15
Abuelita's Sourdough Recipe	18
Time to Go	20
Turtle	22
Solstice	24
Questions for Manuela de Jesus	26
Wrapped	28
Morning Scramble	31
Sweetly Filling: December 2019	32
Pork Tamales Recipe	34

II. Southern Hospitality

Mother Tree Two	38
Brightly Colored Treats	39
Cast Iron	43
Mamo's Famous Southern Fried Chicken Recipe	45
Skates	47
Mirrored	50
Morning Pancakes	51
Hidden	53

Showing Off	55
Sharing Malteds	59
Baking Memories: December 2021	62
Mamo's Fruitcake Recipe	65

III. Home Sweet Home

Mother Tree Three	68
Pies	69
Yellow	71
The Essentials	72
Christmas Morning in the New House	73
Wild Parrot	75
Smoking on Balcony Only	79
Sewn Up	80
Holidaze	83
Pan Dulce	86
Painted	88
Grandma Mary's Empanada Recipe	89
Phone Call	91
Lemon Meringue Pie	93
Ice Cream for Breakfast	95
Fifteen Things I Miss About My Mom	98
Lemon Meringue Pie Recipe	100
Epilogue: The Storyteller	102
Author's Notes	103
Acknowledgments	106

PREFACE

Following are my memories of childhood experiences and interactions with my four grandmothers and my mom. As a storyteller, I have taken the liberty of braiding stories well-known in our family with my personal childhood stories as a way to bring their emotional truths to life. My aunts are composites of one or more individuals. Some names have been changed to respect and guard their privacy. Our family recipes are oral traditions—any inconsistencies in the ingredients or methods are my mistakes.

INTRODUCTION

In the isolation of the 2020 COVID-19 pandemic, I discovered a treasure trove of family stories archived on cassette tapes from the 1970s. To reclaim these stories, I embarked on a reflective journey of childhood. While some memories are rich and full of details, others only produced more questions. Almost all involve the smell, taste, and hands-on making of food. This is how my family gives love to one another: through bread, empanadas, tamales, fried chicken, and lemon meringue pies.

I was raised in a Mexican American cultural community, with influences from the Deep South on my mom's side. These stories explore the intersection of being raised by four grandmas of a mixed cultural lineage and ask the questions: What was shared and what was held back? What are the traditional meals passed down? What are the stories about who we are and where we came from? What lessons and recipes can I pass down to my daughters?

As I began to pack away my baking supplies for an impending kitchen remodel, the stories emerged and transported me back through time and space. From the large metal masa mixing bowl, Mom's glass pie plates, and the tiny metal loaf pans: each one sweeps me up in a wave of joyful, nostalgic memories. I know that my Great-Grandma Mamo's cast-iron pan, in its usual spot on the front burner, will be one of the last items I pack.

In my family, kitchens are the heart of the home. They are the rooms where traditions are created and shared, conversations and storytelling happen, and tiny demonstrations of love are given daily. Mom and my grandmas instilled in me a deep appreciation for all aspects of food and the ways it is woven into our lives, from large family holiday gatherings to the daily meal prep.

In this book, I'm serving up a recipe map of the women of my family. We are the caregivers, the strength, the backbone, and the bakers that sprinkle flour with love to make it all happen.

May these stories feed your soul as they feed mine.

MATRIARCHAL ODE

These are the women who raised me
four grandmas and my mom
cared for me
fed me, clothed me, loved me
one big community

Their stories are our heritage
they baked and cooked their love
between the fluffy masa
in tiny loaves of fruitcake
and whipped in the meringue of the tart lemon pie

They raised their children
in multigenerational homes where
their native tongue became a lost language
they worked in factories and schools
canning fish and serving fish fingers

My mom's generation stepped up to college
and became teachers, nurses, and lawyers
professional women with demanding jobs
juggling childcare and careers
still baking love and tucking hugs
into brown sack lunches

ANCESTORS ASSEMBLE

FOR ALL OUR DAUGHTERS

We are a ragtag crew of survivors. Always lifting and striving to better ourselves to give you this gift: to pass as white, to be accepted as an equal, to be present "in the room where it happens." We worked at canneries, as house cleaners, custodians, and lunch ladies. We scrubbed floors and worked long hours on factory lines. Endless days of backbreaking work. All to reach this point where you can choose how to spend your time so that you can reap the benefits and rewards. To make your mark, teach, research, and strive for the betterment of us all: our family, neighborhood, community, and nation. Stand on the shoulders of your maternal ancestors, and claim our lands and these rights. Fight for reparations. Speak for those still stuck in migration lines at the border, invisible as we once were.

See us, claim us, bring us with you into the light. We stand beneath you, lifting you higher so that you can reach for the brightest stars.

Call on us when you need support and inspiration. We are always here for you!

Theodosia (Abuelita)
Coahuila, Mexico, and Harbor City, California

Mary
Harbor City, California

Minnie (Mamo)
Purcell, Oklahoma, and Lomita, California

May
Lomita, California

Mary
San Pedro, California

I.
LA COCINA

Grandma Mary's Kitchen
Harbor City, California

Mother Tree One

Abuelita
Great-Great-Grandma Theodosia
1884 – 1989

⋮

Great-Grandma Manuela de Jesus
1897 – 1965

⋮

Grandma Mary Josephine
1923 – 1996

⋮

Dad
James
1943 –

⋮

Maria Julie
1966 –

CHRISTMAS EVE TAMALES

Mom puts her hand on my shoulder and nudges me awake.

"Time to get up, sweetie."

Waking immediately, I rush into the bathroom where I laid out my sweats the night before. Christmas Eve: the longest and most exciting day of the year. It's 6:00 a.m. Mom and I are heading out to pick up the masa for family tamale making. We have to get there early before they run out.

The Lincoln Continental glides through the empty streets of San Pedro—we flow onto the freeway at Gaffey Street and off ten minutes later at Bandini Boulevard. As we pull up to the tiny storefront, we are surrounded by a wave of women chattering in Spanish. At age eleven, I'm already at my full height of five feet seven and can easily see over the crowd. I guide my mom to the counter.

"Venticinco libras de masa preparada," my mom tells the clerk. I add a bag of pan dulce and six bags of dry corn husks. I relish the feeling of the warm squishy bags of masa as I slide them into our cloth totes. Hefting the heavy bags, I guide us as we wind our way out.

It's still dark out when we get to the house. Grandma Mary, my father's mom, is in her dark-blue velour bathrobe at the stove. Tiny Abuelita, four feet nine in her slippers, is bustling around gathering ingredients to add to the masa. The sweet-savory fragrance of the pork in chili sauce bubbling on the back burner greets us as soon as we come in the door. Grandma Mary has been cooking the chili and marinating the meat for the tamales all week.

After our familiar greetings and kisses, I slip a red apron over my head.

"Aquí, Mariquita," Abuelita says as she hands me the large metal bowl for mixing the masa.

Even though the masa is preparado, we still knead it: adding lard and chili broth to the mix. As someone with large, strong hands, I was recruited to help mix the masa when I was nine years old.

My aunts and cousins start arriving between 7:00 and 8:00 a.m. By then, I've already mixed one batch of masa to the fluffiness Abuelita demands. She tests it by rolling a small pinch of dough between her fingers and dropping it in a glass of water to see if it floats off the bottom.

"Está lista," she declares. Relieved, I start wiping the excess masa off my hands.

While my aunts and cousins stream in and get settled, I wash my hands and take a pan dulce break. The pink concha crumbles in my hands and mouth and is gone in a few bites.

Out on the enclosed patio, my aunts are setting up the assembly line. My youngest cousins are given the dry corn husks to soak and separate. The masa I've just mixed is divided into smaller bowls and set out with large spoons along the length of the table. The warm pork in chili is at the end near the large steamer pots. Over the next few hours, our group of twenty will collectively make over twelve dozen meat-filled tamales, and five dozen sweet dessert tamales that have raisins, pineapple juice, and brown sugar mixed in.

The bulk of the work is spreading the masa evenly on the corn husks. My aunts laugh and chatter as they work, sharing family news. As they talk, they demonstrate the spreading technique to my younger girl cousins. The boy cousins are never invited, and the uncles wouldn't think to attend.

The chatter at the table quiets down when Aunt Grace asks, "Abuelita, tell us about when you were a girl."

Abuelita begins, "Mi madre murió…"

Aunt Ruth pipes up, "In English!"

Abuelita starts again. "My mother, she died, in childbirth with my little sister. I was maybe five or six. I don't remember my birthday." Everyone chuckles. This has been an ongoing dilemma, trying to figure out my great-great-grandma's birth date. Abuelita continues, "Mi padre estaba triste."

This time Grandma Mary reminds her, "In English, for the little ones, por favor." Even though most of my aunts and Mom are bilingual, my cousins and I have limited Spanish.

Abuelita sighs and tries again, "My father was sad. Difficult to bring us up alone. We all moved to San Antonio, Texas. To be near his aunt." There is a short pause while Abuelita goes to get more chili sauce from the kitchen. Then she continues, "One day we are out having lunch. A family sitting near starts talking to my dad about us kids. They ask if I would like to come with them and learn how to sew. I looked at him. 'Si Papá' I say. I go. I live with this family. It is not so close. I only see my papa and brothers and sisters on weekends. The women in the family sewed dresses and made lace. I worked hard. I was happy to learn. But the sewing business no good. Not enough customers." Abuelita pauses, and Grandma Mary nods in encouragement.

"One day the family decide to move. Back to Mexico City. But no tell my papá. Pack up and move us in the dark of night. No one knows where we go. I don't see my family for ten years or more. I live with these people as if they were my family. Till I get married. To that old man, your great-great-grandpa." She laughs. "That's a different story."

A family stole Abuelita when she was a child? Moved to a new city without telling her dad? My cousins and I look at each other in horror. Could we also be taken?

My mom, seeing the thoughts race across my face, leans over and gives me a half hug, and says, "No one is going to steal you, sweetie," before dropping a kiss on my forehead.

The chatter at the table resumes as Abuelita shuffles back to the kitchen. "Venga Mariquita, time to mix more masa." At these family gatherings, I am always Mariquita, or Little Mary, since both Mom and Grandma are also named Mary.

By noon the first pots are on the stove, and we can take a lunch break. We have cooked some tamales in a smaller pan to eat now. The savory steam of chili and masa envelopes us as we unwrap the first cooked tamales of the day. I add beans from the pot on the back burner and squeeze in at the table. The first bite is warm, spicy, and comforting all at once.

"Abuelita," drawn by Jacob Gutierrez

ROLLING IN THE DOUGH

I smell it as soon as I get out of my parents' car—the pungent warm scent of fresh sourdough rolls. Abuelita is baking! Running inside, I let the screen door slam behind me as I quickly work my way through the obligatory hugs and kisses. First to my grandpa in his recliner, then to my aunts and uncles scattered about on the floral sofas in the living room. Finally, I careen into the kitchen, shouting out, "Abuelita, estoy aquí!"

Today is a special rite of passage: my great-great-grandma is teaching us how to make fresh Easter rolls. Abuelita only makes these rolls, with their crispy crust and soft, squishy insides, once a year.

The big metal mixing bowl is on the table with the flour, salt, shortening, yeast, eggs, and sugar. Abuelita starts by mixing the yeast into the warm water, before showing us how to measure it out and add in the sugar, salt, and eggs. The lard is melting in a pan on the stove and once it's cool it will be added to the wet mixture.

My cousin Tami and I are giggling and chatting about friends at school. My cousin slowly pours the flour, as I knead it into the wet mixture. "Abuelita, can you tell us a story while we mix the dough?"

Abuelita washes her hands and settles onto a chair with a small cup of coffee.

I didn't have many friends. We moved too much. There was this village one time on the outskirts of the town, I lived in a small one-bedroom shack. Besides cleaning, cooking, and laundry there was not much to do. There was a short, squat Indian woman, very nosy. She visited all the locals, gathering tidbits, they called her the Gossip.

So, I invited the Gossip to come over. But most mornings after tea and eating, the Gossip would just fall into a deep sleep. So much that snores rumbled the walls of the shack. Upon awakening, the Gossip would get up and shuffle off, without telling me any news.

After several mornings, frustrated, I decide to play a prank on the Gossip. While she sleeping, I got out my paints and set to it. After the Gossip woke, she shuffled off as usual.

Since the shack had no mirrors, the Gossip did not see her face as she left. Only when she encountered some children on the street, who ran off screaming "Demon lady!"

When the Gossip got home, she looked in the mirror. A ghost on her face! I painted her as a spirit, como "Dia de Los Muertos," and a skeleton stared out.

The Gossip ran out screaming, "Ayudame-estoy muerto!" She ran all over screaming, till one of the women threw water at her. Then the paint ran and the Gossip realized she been tricked. No more visits from the Gossip after that.

With our hands caked in wet dough, we can't wipe the sweet tears off our faces—our cheeks hurt from laughing. I cover the dough with a dish towel, and we go giggling to the sink to wash our hands.

ABUELITA'S SOURDOUGH RECIPE

Ingredients:

½ package yeast (approx. 1 tablespoon)
½ cup water, lukewarm
2 tablespoon lard or Crisco shortening
¼ cup sugar
1 egg
2½ cups flour
¼ teaspoon salt

Instructions:

In a large bowl, mix dry yeast in water, set aside for 10 minutes until it is frothy. In a small pan on low heat, melt lard or shortening, set aside until cool. Add sugar and egg to the yeast and water mixture. Whisk together. Add the cooled melted shortening. Sift the flour in slowly (a cup at a time, adding salt to the second cup of flour) while still stirring the dough. When it is too thick to stir, knead with your hands until dough is smooth. Keep mixing until all the flour is added in. Take dough and slap it against a wooden cutting board. Knead for approximately 5 more minutes, until you can feel the glutenous structure. Put dough into a big bowl to rise, and let it sit for 3 hours. Then pinch palm size (2 to 3 inches across) sections of dough and put them in rows on a baking sheet. Let rest for second rise for 30 minutes under a dry cloth.

Preheat the oven to 350°F. Bake the rolls for about 20 minutes. When they are brown on top, they are done. Makes around a dozen rolls.

TIME TO GO

When Mom said, "It's time to go," I cried in dismay. "No, it's too early. I'm still playing!"

I loved the big family gatherings at Grandma Mary's house—loads of delicious food and being with my cousins, playing endless games of tag and hide-and-seek. We were always hanging out in the backyard, licking popsicles, or splashing on the Slip 'N Slide made from trash bags in the front yard. It was never enough time, and before I knew it my mom would be packing up things in the car and beginning the round of goodbyes. Occasionally I could get a reprieve and con my mom into letting me stay the night if I didn't have homework or chores to do at home.

My mom worked full-time as an elementary school teacher and ran a tight ship. Homework needed to be done before I could play with friends on the block. Every Saturday we would clean the house in a morning frenzy, desperate to finish so that we could head out to play. It always seemed as if we were the only kids on the block with weekly chores and meal prep duties.

As an adult with my own kids, I've come to appreciate my mom's organization and structure. It's a fine line of teaching responsibility, which I balance out with the occasional spontaneous surprise. We do play and go out for donuts and ice cream more than I did when I was a kid. But we also turn the music up on Sunday morning and clean the house in a whirlwind of dusting and vacuuming. Singing along to pop songs, calling out Harry Potter trivia questions, and making the chores a family activity. And when they beg to play longer, I smile as they state their case. We often stay later than I intended, but I don't mind.

Moving up north and being isolated from family, I couldn't give my children regular access to their multitudes of cousins. Instead, I spoil them by cooking our family recipes because food is a huge part of my love language.

TURTLE

It was a quiet summer day at Grandma Mary's. In the living room, Abuelita sat crocheting sets of slippers. It took months to make a pair for each of the grandkids to receive for Christmas. The fan was rotating, slowly pushing the hot summer air back and forth. I lay sprawled on the carpet, waiting for my youngest aunt to get back from her piano lesson. I looked up at Abuelita and pleaded, "Tell me one of your stories, pleassse!"

"Por supuesto, let me finish this." She tied off the yarn at the back of a pair of hot pink slippers. "Have I told you about the turtles?"

Confused, I said, "No, Abuelita, only about the Gossip whose face you painted."

Wiping her thick, Coke-bottle glasses with a hanky from her sweater pocket, she began:

> *When I married your great-great-grandfather, it was just a jungle where we lived. I was terrible and bored; I was so young—I didn't know what to do with myself. I couldn't crochet, I couldn't*

sew, I couldn't do nothing. I had no thread, no needle. I had to do something.

We lived in a place where there was a big river. There was alligators and crocodiles. And there were big turtles. They would come and lay down there where it was soft on the banks of the river. Every day one turtle come and lay with her little baby turtles. After having the sun, she was trying to get to the river. I took my foot and press on her back, and I took the knife and cut the head, and the feet, and everything. I put it in a pot to boil. So that I could see what turtle meat tastes like.

The little turtles came out hunting for their mother. They went to the river and swam away. Then I think, I'm going to give everybody in the village turtle meat to eat. I never cooked turtle, so I put it in the pot and left it. Later I go divide it up—and that turtle was moving! The turtle I killed and boiled for three hours still was moving in the bucket. I got scared and didn't eat nothing.

My mouth dropped open. "You killed the mama turtle?"

Abuelita nodded. "Si, la maté."

I pressed on. "And it was still moving after you cooked it?"

Throwing her hands up, Abuelita said, "Maybe it was a ghost, come haunt me."

Stunned, I fell back silent on the braided rug, splayed in the heat.

SOLSTICE

Digging down
up to my elbows
deep in the dirt
of my summer garden.

Offering tribute,
planting the Three Sisters:
Native traditional vegetables
that support and nourish each other.

Grandma Mary ran off
with a Mexican migrant worker
after a solstice harvest dance.
Theodosia, the matriarch, tracked and
dragged them back to San Pedro

To a small one-room house:
Theodosia worked at the cannery,
Grandpa worked at the Docks,
and Mary cooked and raised ten kids,
my dad the eldest.

Shaking the roots free,
I plant the seedlings
together on a mound:
squash, tomatoes, and beans
intertwined so they can flourish.

QUESTIONS FOR MANUELA DE JESUS

Before you were stolen at the age of fifteen, did you sing and dream of big adventures? Did you stash your secret wishes in a hope chest? Were you betrothed to another landowner's son? Was your future mapped out at birth? Why were you in the field unchaperoned that day? Had you heard about the Pancho Villa raids and abductions in the nearby villages? Did you know Papa Jesus before he rode through the fields and carried you away? Did something unspoken pass between you in a single gaze? Did you reach up to embrace the escape from your corseted life? Did you fight against it? Did you swoon at the fantasy of being a stolen bride? Were you resigned to whatever fate took you that day? Did you write to your family to tell them about your twelve love children and your life on the farm? Did your mother disown you? Sever all contact with you? Did you ever officially marry Papa Jesus? Were you happy? The one photo I have shows a joyful scrunched-up smile in the sunlight. What did you tell your daughters when they asked how you met

Papa? When strangers came riding up, did you call your daughters inside and hold them close to your bosom? Or did you plant them like sunflowers in the field, ripe for plucking, as you once were?

WRAPPED

It's a sunny summer day in Southern California when I burst into the bright lime-green kitchen. Grandma Mary is in her usual spot next to the stove. The smell of pinto beans bubbling on the back burner mingles with the aroma of slightly singed tortillas.

I reach my arms around Grandma's soft, doughy middle. After a peck on the cheek, she hands me a warm tortilla with a pat of butter melting inside. "Hola mija! I haven't seen you, what have you been up to?"

As I chew my tortilla, I softly mutter, "I was in a play at summer camp."

"How was the show?" Grandma asks.

I look around to see if any of my cousins are nearby. "It was kind of embarrassing…"

"I'm sure you were wonderful. Dime mas," Grandma prompts as she pats out more tortillas. I settle at the table, wrapping my lanky limbs in and around the wooden chair legs, and begin.

The elementary school auditorium was packed. You should have seen it—every seat was taken; there were even people sitting in the aisles. The

> *play was Snow White, Rose Red. We were all cast and crew. During the six weeks of camp, we learned our lines, built sets, and found costumes. My best friend, Jill, was the narrator. I played the prince.*

"That sounds lovely," Grandma encourages. I continue, slightly louder.

> *The play was going well. We were near the end. I was nervously standing backstage when Jill boomed out, "And then the bear became a prince!" So I came out to center stage but couldn't open the zipper on Mom's fake fur coat. Jill repeated, slower, "And...then...the...bear...became... a... prince."*
>
> *I flung myself about, still wrestling with the zipper, and the audience started to laugh.*

In the kitchen, I mime my struggle with the coat. My cousins are peeking in from the backyard. Encouraged, I raise my voice even more.

> *Jill looked at me and pointed. "And then the BEAR became a PRINCE!" Inside the coat, I was sweating. I had trouble breathing. The zipper was glued shut. My face was bright red. I wanted the show to be over. I wanted off the stage.*

Now I am writhing and flopping around on the kitchen floor, demonstrating my struggle with the coat. My aunts and uncles are looking on and laughing from the living room, while my cousins are huddled in a giggling mass by the back door. I yell out the ending.

> *Everyone in the auditorium was laughing loudly as I slithered around on the stage floor in the brown coat. Jill shouted, "THE BEAR BECOMES A PRINCE!" just as I pull the coat up and off over my head to a roaring standing ovation.*

"Ta-da!" I throw my hands in the air and cheers erupt as everyone crowds into the kitchen, hugging and congratulating me. Smiling shyly, I lean forward and melt into Grandma Mary's warm hug.

MORNING SCRAMBLE

It's the end of college winter break, and it's cold and dark at 4:45 a.m. I tromp downstairs, wrapping my robe tightly around me. I only have a few minutes before my youngest leaves for her flight back to Boston. I put on my red apron and with a quick flick of my wrist, I turn on the burner. I grab eggs, veggies, chorizo, and flour tortillas from the fridge. The eggs sizzle as I scramble the mixture in the cast-iron pan.

The spicy tang stirs up memories of Grandma Mary at the stove. Day or night, she was always on hand to whip up hot breakfast burritos for us. She would throw in whatever was in the fridge: potatoes, hot dogs, beans, chorizo, and eggs. While Grandma Mary used the real chorizo, with its bright red color and mysterious bits of gristle, I cook with soy-based chorizo. Same taste, less mystery.

I wrap the burritos in paper towels. Sadly, I shuffle around cleaning the kitchen counter, waiting for a goodbye kiss from Mac. My little one flies solo now.

SWEETLY FILLING: DECEMBER 2019

Christmas in Seattle is a quiet holiday, just us four. Pajamas and books on Christmas Eve, presents and pancakes on Christmas morning. Tamale making is scheduled with neighbors and friends on a day between Christmas and New Year's.

I order the masa by phone and drive down to Burien to pick it up, fifteen miles south on I-5. You can choose between corn or masa harina, but it all is preparada. When I get the masa home, I divide out a bit and set it aside for the sweet tamales. Then I follow Abuelita's instructions, adding chili broth, shortening, and a pinch of salt. I knead the masa till it fluffs up and floats off the bottom of a water glass.

The neighbors arrive bearing pre-made fillings: verde chili with chicken, roasted serrano chilis, and ranchero cheese. I cook the red chili sauce with pork, mimicking the steps Grandma Mary taught me as a girl. I put on my red apron and pass out extras to the neighbors. I pause and remember childhood family gatherings with all my aunts and cousins around the long table. The bright chatter brings me back, I look lovingly at my neighbors and friends, they are my extended family here.

My daughter Riley is happy to help mix the masa, her hands so much like my own. My girls love to help assemble the tamales. Riley takes charge of making the sweet tamales, adding in raisins, pineapple, and even chocolate chips, which her younger sister, Mac, playfully steals and eats by the handful.

We gossip about kids, jobs, and other neighborhood news as we spread the masa.

"I heard that Sanchez is looking to sell his house and move south," Melinda shares. The group collectively gasps. "Oh no! But we love the potluck dishes he shares at our monthly dinners," Mac exclaims.

Melinda spouts her familiar refrain, "No one else is allowed to leave the neighborhood!"

I laugh, "We aren't moving, I'm finally getting my kitchen remodeled after twenty years!"

Within a couple of hours, all the masa is spread, and the steaming pots are full. Each person takes a couple back to their own home for the two- to three-hour cook time. We will meet back here later to taste and divide up the cooked tamales. After cleanup, the girls and I collapse onto the nearest sofa. In soft exhaustion, we cuddle and read our Christmas books, while the sweet smell of tamales tantalizes us.

PORK TAMALES RECIPE

Ingredients:

    2.5 pounds pork loin
    1 large can (28 ounces) enchilada sauce
    1 bag dry corn husks (50 to 75 husks)
    5 pounds masa preparado
        (set aside 1 pounds for sweet tamales)
    1 cup Crisco shortening
    Pinch of salt
    ¼ cup pork broth
    ¼ cup vegetable broth

Preparing the filling:

Using an Instant Pot, braise the pork on each side on the sauté function for about 10 minutes. Then cook the pork loin on the pressure cook function for 30 minutes. Let it sit and warm for another 30 minutes. Take the pork out and cut/tear it into thin strips. Return the pork to the pot and add the enchilada sauce. Let simmer for 2 to 3 hours, then cool and refrigerate until you are ready to make the tamales. Before rewarming, skim off the clumps of fat from the surface and set aside to mix in with the masa. Separate the pork from the excess broth.

Making the tamales:

Separate and soak the corn husks in warm water. Once pliable and clean, place them to dry on dish towels, making sure that they are spread out. Cut shortening and reserved skimmed fat into the masa batter. Add salt, warm veggie broth, and pork broth as you knead the masa dough. To determine when the masa is ready for spreading, roll a pinch of masa into a ball and place it gently into a glass of water. If the masa floats slightly off the bottom of the glass, then the masa is ready for spreading. If it does not rise, add a bit more broth and continue kneading.

Take a spoonful of masa and, starting at the wide end of a husk, spread upward to the narrow top end. Try to cover most of the husk, to both edges, thinning gradually as you spread upwards. Fill generously with pork, draining the extra liquid off. Fold the sides of the masa-covered husks horizontally over the meat, overlapping each other, and then fold in half vertically. Drain off any excess sauce back into the pot with the pork filling.

In a inner colander or use a steaming basket set in a large metal pot, place the filled husks upright around an inverted mug or large glass and cook. Add enough water to cover the bottom of the pot, but not touching the tamales. Steam for 45 to 60 minutes. Remove from heat and let rest for at least 10 minutes before serving.

For sweet tamales:

Add pineapple juice, brown sugar, raisins, and shredded coconut to the masa preparado. Put a tablespoon of the masa onto a scrap of corn husk, and then wrap and tie it up. The sweet tamales steam in a half-hour or so.

II. SOUTHERN HOSPITALITY

Mamo's Kitchen
Lomita, California

Mother Tree Two

Mamo
Great-Grandma Minne Gertrude
1898 – 1990

⋮

Grandma (Eula) May
1922 – 1985

⋮

Mom
Mary Gertrude
1944 – 2010

⋮

Maria Julie
1966 –

BRIGHTLY COLORED TREATS

Into the kitchen I run, chasing my brother. My great-grandma, Mamo, reaches out and grabs me, spinning me towards the sink.

"Wash your filthy paws. We've got work to do," she scolds.

Quickly, I glance over to check my mom's expression. She's unpacking bags of nuts and candies onto the table and pays Mamo no mind.

Grandma May, my mom's mother, comes in and slams the back door. It's tight in the tiny kitchen. The baking supplies are piled on the table and counter. I slide into my usual place, next to the wall. At age nine, I'm happy to be included for the first time in the annual fruit cake preparation. Picking up a knife, I struggle to follow my mom's clean movements. It's difficult keeping the tip of the knife down while rotating and slicing the blade through the walnuts, as Mom does so effortlessly.

Mamo is working quietly at the stove mixing the dough. Grandma May has the difficult task of chopping the candied cherries and pineapple slices. I sneak some of the candies to chew on as I chop.

Grandma May notices the theft and chuckles, "You always liked brightly colored treats. There was that time I was watching you…"

Dust motes gleamed and danced above the small black-and-white television. I sat cross-legged in my jammies on the green shag carpet. My grandma's dog, Puddles, hoovered up the spilled Cheerios around me. A mutt, he looked like a small step stool or footrest. When he was out of floor snacks, Puddles sighed and plopped down next to me.

On the TV, the zany antics of Bugs Bunny bled into the explosive violence of the Road Runner.

"Beep beep," I echoed. A horn honked and I glanced out the window, nope, not Mama.

On the coffee table was my brand-new box of sixty-four crayons. So many shiny candy colors sparkled in the sunlight. Slowly I opened the box and began distributing them into piles: one for me, one for Puddles. With my chubby toddler fingers, I broke each crayon into tiny, bite-size pieces. Did the red ones taste like berries?

When my mom returned from her appointment, she took in the empty wrappers and stubs of crayons lying about. I lifted my arms and beamed up at my mom with a wide red, waxy grin as Grandma May walked in from the kitchen.

Now Grandma May guffaws and coughs, bringing my attention back to the kitchen where I stand with a knife in my hand.

Grandma continues, "I said to your mom, 'Your little artist is going to be shitting rainbows for the next week.'" She snorts and points at me with her unlit cigarette before heading out back for a smoke break, "And you sure did!"

In the wake of the story, Mom notices I've stopped chopping nuts. My hands are cramped from holding the handles of the blade too tight, and I flex my fingers to relax them.

"Why don't you prep the baking tins now?" she suggests, sensitive as always to my feelings.

Mom hands me a stack of three-by-five-inch tins and a stick of butter. I line the tins like soldiers on the green linoleum of the kitchen counter. Absorbed in this mindless task, my shoulders drop, and I start humming softly to myself.

After looking to confirm that Grandma May is still smoking out back, Mom pulls out a bottle of brandy and covers the dry fruit with it. The strong whiff of alcohol makes me cringe and gag. After soaking the fruit, Mom puts the brandy back behind the cans of Campbell's mushroom soup. Grandma May hates mushrooms and won't move those cans anytime soon. When Mom sees me watching, she puts a finger to her lips and winks.

The rest of the day passes in a hazy blur as we continue to chop, soak, and mix batter for what seems like hundreds of small baking tins. They are moved in and out of the oven in batches of ten, then rushed out to the patio to cool. Finally, they are wrapped in red cellophane with gold ribbon bows, ends curled with scissors, like Shirley Temple's sausage curls. Just like the curls I had as a toddler.

CAST IRON

My great-grandma Mamo was a hard woman. She had strong hands, gnarled from arthritis; a piercing, steely blue-eyed gaze; and a sharp tongue that lashed out at us all. That is, everyone except my mother, who was her favorite grandchild and the only person Mamo allowed to help in the kitchen.

The kitchen was Mamo's domain, and the cast-iron fry pan her most prized possession. It sat on the front burner, gleaming with oil and ready for pancake flipping on weekend sleepovers. After breakfast, Mamo would dip a slice of Wonder Bread through the drippings and devour it between bites of raw onion—eaten like a ripe apple—one crunchy bite at a time. Fried chicken, seared in the frying pan, was the star of Sunday dinners, featured with enough side dishes to feed a small, hungry army: okra, black-eyed peas, green beans, and ambrosia salad.

I remember the tenderness with which Mamo handled and cleaned that pan, as gentle as if it were a newborn infant. Mom eventually inherited the fry pan and all its culinary secrets. But Mom was more of a casserole (one and done) type of cook, and the pan took shelter in the warming oven. When Mom passed away ten years ago, I bundled up the pan and took it home to Seattle. I put it back out in the place of honor on the front right burner of my stove. Daily, I cook in the skillet: breakfast scrambles, sauté veggies, and pan-fried chicken.

Recently, my daughter Mac was home on a break from college. Cleaning the skillet after breakfast, she asked, "Can I have this when I get married?"

> Always out and nesting on the front burner
> sometimes gleaming after a cleaning
> or full of milky white fat drippings
> that Mamo would run a slice of Wonder
>   Bread through
> then pop in her mouth

> The skillet was in constant use
> from bacon frying and pancake flipping
> on weekend sleepovers
> to fried chicken
> perfectly crispy outside, tender inside
> for our "Southern" Sunday dinner

> Watching her lovingly clean the pan
> strong, gnarled hands gently
> sprinkling rock salt and wiping with a rag—
> not rough, the way she scrubbed
> my sun-darkened knees with Ajax

MAMO'S FAMOUS SOUTHERN FRIED CHICKEN RECIPE

Ingredients:

2 fryer chickens, cut into pieces
4 cups buttermilk
5 cups flour
3 tablespoons Lawry's Seasoned Salt
2 teaspoons paprika
2 teaspoons black pepper
½ cup whole milk
2 eggs
Lard or Crisco for frying

Instructions:

Rinse chicken pieces in cold water, pat dry, place in a bowl, and cover with buttermilk. Soak in the fridge overnight. Take chicken out and let come to room temperature. Whisk dry ingredients together in a large bowl. Whisk milk and eggs together, then slowly add to the flour mixture while continuing to whisk. Stir till smooth. Heat a scoop of lard or Crisco in a cast-iron skillet. Coat the chicken in the wet breading and stage on a platter. Fry the pieces, 3 to 4 at a time, leaving space between them. Turn over as needed. Cook on medium heat till the outside is crispy brown, and there is no evidence of pink juice or meat. Thighs and breasts will need longer cooking time. Drain fried pieces on paper towels, then place covered on a platter in a warm oven until ready to serve.

SKATES

We drove down the long driveway—yellow, red, and pink gladiolus were lined up like soldiers on the side. The sweet and savory aroma of dinner was already wafting out, enveloping the entire lawn, and circling the tiny white house.

Whenever my family walked into the kitchen for the weekly Sunday afternoon dinner, the tiny aluminum kitchen table was laden with food. The serving dishes overflowed with various side dishes of green beans, mashed potatoes, sweet yams, salad, cornbread, and gravy. But the star of the meal was Mamo's fried chicken, golden and glittering on a serving platter near the stove.

My brother, Jesse, three years younger and small for his age, crawled under the table to his seat. I turned sideways and squeezed in to sit against the wall. Mamo always sat next to the stove, so she could jump up and get extras if we ran out. I always had to taste a little bit of everything, including the three desserts: Sara Lee chocolate cake, peach cobbler, and fudge. When the time came, I refused seconds, feeling a bit like a stuffed turkey.

That day, as a gift for my ninth birthday, my great-grandma Mamo gave me a pair of roller derby skates. At age seventy-six, Mamo was a dedicated derby fan. After Sunday dinners she watched the bouts broadcast by KTLA, her favorite being the women's Los Angeles Thunderbirds, also known as the LA T-Birds. I looked up in surprise after opening the box. The bright blue skates were in T-Bird colors with red and white stripes. The clear red polyurethane wheels gleamed. The skates were the nicest present she had ever given me.

During the games, Mamo would scream at the blockers to pummel "those low-life, yellow-bellied scum!" She would cheer for the jammer to ricochet in front, thus racking up the most points and winning the bout for the team.

I sat quietly, teasing the brown shag carpet between my fingers. Looking up from my Nancy Drew book, I watched with a mixture of awe and revulsion as the derby players raced around the sloped track. I cringed when they elbowed and shoved each other over the railings. I looked at my shiny new skates in horror. *Did Mamo expect* me *to become a derby player?*

After the game, I tried on the skates. I spun in slow circles in the garage while continuing to read. The stacked boxes and gardening tools crowded in on me, but it was the only smooth surface for skating on. Suddenly, Mamo opened the side door, backlit by the bright sunshine. Startled, I dropped my book and fell to the concrete with my coltish legs flung out, wheels still spinning. Mamo huffed in disgust and turned back to the house.

That night, I hid my new skates in the back of my closet. When my mom asked about them, I told her they didn't fit.

MIRRORED

Mamo struggles to plait my hair
I suck in my breath
suppressing the pain of each tug
till I pull back and get a slap.

"Ouch, that hurts!"
I meet her steel gaze
in the beveled mirror
and slink back down,
trying to disappear.

Mamo tugs again at the ends,
struggling to tighten the red elastic bands
with her arthritic hands—
fingers curved and folded over
as the branches of the crab apple tree.

While she smooths my fly-away hairs,
I look at her strong profile in the mirror
and our images briefly overlay—
maybe Mamo looked like me
when she was young.

MORNING PANCAKES

Swimming up through the darkness of the early morning light, you follow the sound of percolating bubbles to the kitchen. Your great-grandma Mamo is at the stove, as she is every morning. Pouring batter in silver-dollar-sized dollops, she continues flipping them till they are golden brown. Mamo then slides them onto a white china platter in the oven to keep warm.

Silently, you slip into your usual seat against the wall, cringing as the table squeaks on the linoleum floor. Seeking to blend in with the wallpaper you bow your head over your book, letting your dark-brown hair fall over your face. You peek up when Grandma May stumbles by, fumbling with her smokes and lighter, as she heads out to the back porch.

You steady your breathing to match the ticking of the bright yellow kitchen wall clock. The enticing pancake smells linger in the air, but you refrain from asking for a taste. Mamo's rule: no one can eat until your brother, the golden boy, awakens. Grandma May flops into the chair next to the back door.

"What you reading now?" she asks in her slurred Southern raspy drawl.

You glance up and whisper from behind the veil of hair. "My new Nancy Drew book, *The Hidden Staircase*."

Grandma May nods as she begins shuffling a deck of cards. Your stomach gives a low rumble, May winks and slips you butterscotch candy. She plays solitaire as you both continue to sit and wait.

HIDDEN

Everything about my Grandma May remains veiled behind a smokey haze. Looking through the old black-and-white photo albums, May is always at the edge of the group, blending into the background. I peer closely. What secrets are hidden behind those grey-green eyes and painted-on quizzical brows?

There are no photos of Grandma May's childhood. It is as if she was born fully formed on the half-shell at age twenty when she became a war bride. The post-WWII photos show Grandma May and her sisters with their husbands back from the war. Front and center, Grandma holds my mom lovingly in her arms, a sweet, upturned smile on her red lips.

In the following pages, May shifts to the sidelines, out of focus. So many posed photos of my mom and her three younger sisters: stiff in their starched dresses, all with glasses and bad perms, it's hard to differentiate who is who beyond their heights. Grandma May holds herself remote and isolated, an extra in her own life.

But in my childhood, Grandma May was larger-than-life. In her practical elastic-waistband slacks and colorful tops, she was always up for running around and playing card games. I loved her jokes and enjoyed having her at the children's table in the kitchen, never understanding why my aunts placed her there, and what that meant in terms of family social dynamics.

Almost all my memories of Grandma May involve her smoking. The smoke was always present; I could smell it on her clothes when we hugged.

I still see her alone on the balcony. Her silhouette is framed by the fading light: tight, wavy auburn hair, one thin arm wrapped hugging herself, as the other extends. I still see the red glowing tip of her endless cigarette, the rest of her hidden in haze.

SHOWING OFF

Everyone is in the living room when we arrive. After a round of cursory air kisses, I settle into an armchair, eager to continue reading *The Hobbit*. The quiet conversations of my aunts and their work troubles float around me.

Before I can even finish a chapter, Aunt Georgie announces, "Find your places, dinner is served."

Automatically, I go around the corner to the kitchen, heading to where the kids' table always is. Four place settings of colorful plastic cups and plates are laid out.

"I set the table all by myself," my little cousin announces. A tiny bouquet of hand-picked daisies stands proudly in the middle.

Grandma May shuffles over and settles into the chair closest to the front door. "I guess you all get the pleasure of my company again today," she slurs.

From the dining room, we hear the clink of crystal wine glasses as the adults have a holiday toast. We raised our plastic cups, too.

Grandma May shouts, "Down the hatch!" I pass the sparkling cider around, but Grandma heads to the kitchen to refill her glass.

Between smoke breaks, Grandma entertains us with off-color jokes and stories from her sorting job at Goodwill. She tells us about all the crazy things she's found while sorting clothes, everything from jewelry to "girlie photos," she snorts.

While clearing the table, I overhear my aunts and uncles talking about politics, and arguing about gas rationing. Desperate to change the subject, Mom looks at the black-and-white photos on the wall and asks, "When did you get those framed?" Aunt Georgie embarks on a lengthy explanation. I slip around the corner to look closer.

In one of the photos, Grandma May is seated on a throne with a rhinestone crown. Two leggy showgirls are hovering on either side in matching leotards, dark lipstick, and upswept hair. A man is playfully sniffing one of the long-stemmed red roses on her lap. Grandma poses, head high, a sly upturned smile on her lips.

"Can you tell me about this one?" I request.

Georgie says, "Let me think. It was a cold winter day, 1952, I believe. Your grandma, Eula May, filled out a three-by-five wish card in line at NBC television studio. Out of two thousand possible applicants, she was chosen with twenty others to go onstage and be interviewed by the game show host, Jack Bailey. Somehow, she made the cut to be a finalist, one of four contestants to tell their story live in front of the studio audience.

"I remember watching it at home. Lou was very young and was sitting on Daddy's lap. It was so strange to be watching Mommy on our small black-and-white TV. When it was Mommy's turn, Bailey gently encouraged her to share her story." The story, as Georgie tells it, goes something like this:

> *May started in a slow stutter and then speeds on: "Four girls, two years apart, ages two to eight: MaryGeorgieBetsyLou. Black-and-white saddle shoes, Catholic school fees and uniforms, and always those hungry mouths to feed. Husband out of work, broken arm and leg, a fall while working on the docks. He served in the big one, World War II. Vincent did his duty, doctor bills are adding up, little birds always chirping for more. What's a mother to do? What can she give her four sweet girls for Christmas?"*
>
> *Each item listed off in her Southern drawl, till the audience explodes with claps and cheers, sending the Applause Meter swinging in her favor.*
>
> *The Announcer proclaimed: Tonight's winner is Eula May from Lomita, California. The showgirls gave her a bouquet of roses and guided her to the throne.*

Georgie concludes, "A big truck arrived a couple of weeks later. There were bikes, a wagon, and four baby dolls. Then they pulled off a La-Z-Boy recliner, a GE washer, and boxes and boxes of Hormel chili. We were so surprised!"

Looking closely at the photo, I'm trying to see the Grandma I know, when she staggers in.

Grandma May bellows, "'Queen for a Day,' what a bunch of malarky. But I sure gave 'em a show!" She poses regally in the kitchen archway, chin held high, sparks flying from her grey-green eyes.

SHARING MALTEDS

Grandma May was our playmate whenever my brother and I went for sleepovers at her and Mamo's house. We spent time on the floor building pillow forts, or in the kitchen where she taught us how to make fudge. The weekend was a blur of watching cartoons, playing games, and running in the yard. Growing up, Grandma May was my "fun" grandma. She was always up for anything, from playing hide-and-seek, to endless hours of war, Uno, and other card games. She would lead us in whooping and hollering around the living room until she collapsed on the sofa, short of breath.

But our field trips were the best. I gathered our trekking supplies—army men, bandanas, and my doll, Peaches—into my tiny backpack. My brother grabbed his red felt cowboy hat and holster and put on his boots. All for just a short five-block walk to the local hot dog hut.

My brother was always decked out in his cowboy attire, including his hand-embroidered cowboy shirt made by Mom. Preferring to take on the role of a tracker, I liked to braid my hair and stick feathers in it. On the walk, we would check the bushes, trees, and driveways for assorted wild animals and outlaws. Grandma May joined in, jumping out of bushes to scare us. Lost in our fantasy play, it often took us an hour to get to Wienerschnitzel.

Thirsty and hungry, we struggled to look over the high counter as Grandma May ordered. The workers looked so professional and important in their matching hats and red T-shirts. It was a marvel to watch them as they scooped our chocolate ice cream into a cup, then put it on the old-fashioned silver shake machine where it shimmied and danced.

I can still remember the taste of those thin crispy fries dipped into the thick chocolate malt shakes.

Remember

Grandma, do you remember?

Eating Cheerios in front of the T.V. with me

Coming over early on Christmas morning to help us open the presents under the tree

Teaching me how to rollerskate on my creaky metal wheels

Doing the "Indian War Dance" in a fit of delightful squeals

Making chocolate mousse which was-oh-so very sweet

Helping me make doll plaques for my mom as a special treat

The trips we took to Disneyland where I made you go on all the scary rides

The vacations to San Felipe where we'd watch the changing tides

Reading romance novels which we dutifully exchanged

Playing "Blackjack" and "Crazy Eights" and all the other card games

The times you came and cared for me when I was ill

How you would tease me and call me your little pill

Showing me how to latch hook rugs while I was sick with the chicken pox

All the winter nights we sat cuddled in our bathrobes and warm socks

Thank you, Grandma, for all these things we've shared.

I will always remember!

Written for my grandma who died on October 11, 1985

By María Julie Gutiérrez

Written as a eulogy for Grandma May in 1985.

BAKING MEMORIES: DECEMBER 2021

1. My daughters, Riley and Mac, have just returned from college for winter break. "Let's bake our favorite recipes from the grandmas for our holiday swap," I suggest.

2. I pull down my mom's painted colorful five-by-seven-inch recipe box. Each category overflows with recipes—handwritten, typed, as well as some cut out of magazines and newspapers. After searching through all the cake recipes, I can't find what I'm looking for: Mamo's Fruitcake recipe.

3. I continue the search and look at the recipes behind "Breads," "Cookies," and "Holiday Treats," but I still don't find it. I text my aunt Hannah. Nope, she doesn't have that recipe. I email my aunt Georgie. I wait for a reply. A couple of days later Georgie sends me the recipe. As the foodie of the family, she has lots of advice on how to improve the recipe. I send off a quick thanks and print out the original.

4. The ingredient list calls for three different types of nuts and three kinds of candied fruits. Mamo used to buy these specialty items at her local drugstore, Camelot on 156th in Lomita. They were stocked with the decorative tins on the seasonal aisle, across from the candy for stocking stuffers.

5. The recipe doesn't specify a type of brandy, so I opt for a French brand with low alcohol content. While at the liquor store, I try to buy peppermint schnapps for my mom's Frozen Mint Fangoes recipe, but everyone is out of peppermint due to supply chain shortages.

6. When I get home, I put the candied fruit in a mason jar and generously pour the brandy over them to soak. Aunt Hannah says you can soak them for a day to a month. I put the jar in the fridge until baking day and slip the remainder of the brandy up over the stove.

7. I can't find the tiny five-by-seven disposable baking tins Mamo used, or the red cellophane she wrapped them in. We opt to use bread loaf pans and cut the fruitcake into slices for our holiday platters.

8. On baking day, Mac delights in sucking on brandy-soaked candied fruit as she chops the nuts. Riley is all business—aproned up, with her baking supplies at hand, she is sifting the flour, stirring the batter, and gently folding in the nuts

and candied fruits. After pouring the batter into the tins, she presses the nuts and candies down gently to keep them from rising to the surface.

9. While the little cakes are slow cooking on low heat (200 degrees for two-plus hours), we rifle through the recipe box for additional holiday favorites. The sweet smell of fruitcake fills every corner of our small kitchen.

MAMO'S FRUITCAKE RECIPE

Ingredients:

1 cup sugar
1 cup butter
6 eggs
2 cups flour
1½ cups candied cherries
1½ cup candied pineapple
1 cup pecans
1 cup blanched almonds
1 cup black walnuts
1 cup walnuts
1½ cups coconut snow or finely processed coconut
1½ cup golden raisins
scant teaspoon salt
½ cup brandy

Instructions:

In a large bowl, cream sugar and butter. Beat eggs well and add to sugar and butter mixture, along with the flour. Coarsely chop the candied fruit and nuts and mix with coconut and raisins. Add salt. Pour brandy over and blend well, set aside for two hours (or make up the night before). Add chopped fruit and nuts to the batter gradually to evenly blend all ingredients. Grease 4" x 6" loaf pans and line with parchment paper. Bake for 40 minutes at 350°F. Let cool before removing from pans.

III. HOME SWEET HOME

Mary's House
San Pedro, California

Mother Tree Three

Mom
Mary Gertrude
1944 – 2010

⋮

Maria Julie
1966 –

⋮

Riley **Mac**
2000 – *2003 –*

PIES

"When I first got married, I couldn't cook," my mom explains to the gathering of nieces and nephews on the floor around her feet.

"Papa was in art school, and I was working for the phone company. Money was tight." She pauses while she gestures, holding her thumb and index finger an inch apart.

"But you could get ten pies for a dollar at the store, tiny frozen pot pies. I'd throw them in the oven and that's what we had for dinner every night," She giggles and waits. As an elementary school teacher, she knows how to captivate kids and draw them in. "Till Papa got fed up and said, 'No more pot pies!'" she says using a gruff deep voice. "Go to my mom's and learn to cook. *Please!*' So I did!" she exclaims throwing up her arms.

Mom continues, "The only thing I could cook when we met in high school was a lemon meringue pie." *Aaaaah*—a collective sigh! Everyone loves my mom's pie.

"Pie was the one thing I could make from start to finish. Grandma May never taught us to cook, we only helped assemble the meal in bits and pieces; snap the peas, wash the lettuce, strain the beans." She looks off in the distance for a moment, until one of the kids tugs her back.

"But Mamo taught me how to bake and we all know that Papa loves pie." She laughs and asks, "Remember the story of how he ate his entire birthday pie?"

I turn off the cassette tape and wipe my eyes. It's bittersweet to hear Mom's singsong voice and laughter again after ten-plus years.

YELLOW

The bright walls of our kitchen are sunshine color. Eagerly, I shovel another bite of banana into my mouth. My brother is in his highchair, picking up Cheerios one by one with his stubby toddler fingers. The big yellow box is on the table, just out of reach.

Our small metal table is nestled in the corner, just past the stove. I sit with my back against the wall so I can look out the side-door window, always watching for visiting relatives or friends to stop by.

Mama takes small steps back and forth between the sink and stove. After cooking the lemon custard, she gets out the mixer to make the meringue.

"Can I lick the beater?" I ask.

"Me too!" Jesse shouts.

"Ouch," Mama exclaims, as she turns and bumps into the fridge. Rubbing her elbow, she explains, "I don't know how your Grandma Mary managed in this tiny kitchen with six kids, Abuelita, and a parade of visiting relatives. I'll be happy when the new house is finished."

I nod and smile, basking in the warmth of the cozy kitchen, waiting for my treat.

THE ESSENTIALS

I remember
blue chip stamp booklets,
saving leftovers from Sunday dinners,
hand-me-down clothes,
one pair of shoes for the school year.

But we always had a home,
three meals a day,
camping trips to San Felipe,
once a year visits to Disneyland,
and a Santa present under the tree.

Our small one-bedroom house
2525 Denison,
halfway down the alley,
next door to the local family cemetery.
The kitchen was a tight squeeze for just us four.

But nothing compared to when my dad was a kid
when the kids would eat in shifts
wolfing down single servings of
rice, beans, and tortillas
and fighting over any extras.

Always wanting more.

CHRISTMAS MORNING IN THE NEW HOUSE

The bitter, burnt smell of percolated coffee wafts into my new bedroom. Sunlight is just beginning to creep around the edges of the bright, colorful curtains Mom sewed. Squinting, I struggle to change the dark shadows into recognizable shapes. *Am I at Mamo's house for a sleepover?* Rubbing my eyes, I realize I'm in the wooden bed Dad made me. Feeling all my dolls lined up next to me and *click*, suddenly I remember!

Hopping out of bed, I rush across the hall to wake my brother. He has his own room now in the new house, but some nights I still find him snoring under my bed. "Wake up! It's Christmas!" I nudge him awake and pull him out from under the quilt. Together we race through the empty dining room and barrel into the bright living room. Mom hasn't had time to make the curtains yet.

Mamo and Grandma May are perched on our stiff new orange-plaid folding couch sipping coffee and quietly chatting with Mama. Our small five-foot-tall tree is glittering in the corner near the floor-to-ceiling front windows. Its spindly branches are haphazardly decorated with paper and Play-Doh ornaments that we made last week. A small pile of colorful wrapped packages circles the tree, and a couple of presents sit on the coffee table in front of my grandmas.

Everything twinkles in the early morning sunlight, but I only have eyes for one thing. Frantically, I peer around the edges of the branches till I spot a gleam of chrome—the handlebar of my new bike! It isn't wrapped, there's just a giant red bow and a tag from Santa.

I roll the bright pink bike out from behind the tree. I admire its sparkly tassels and colorful banana seat. After hopping on for a quick picture, I go to ride it. The empty living and dining room stretch out in front of me, as big as our previous backyard.

But, before I can push down the pedal, Mom intercedes. "Take it outside, sweetie."

Grandma May comes with me, running beside me as I strive to balance on two wheels. She stays with me till I am flying up the street, wind whipping my hair. Eager to show my best friend, Sue, my new bike, I pedal up the hill. Standing in front of the house, Grandma May has lit a cigarette and is gazing into the distance as I cycle away.

WILD PARROT

It's 2:29 p.m. I bounce quietly in my seat as I watch the clock. The minute hand sweeps backward?! *Aaaagh!* But then it swings forward in a whoosh, and the dismissal bell rings. *Yay, school's out!*

Amongst the clamoring students, I search for my neighbor and best friend, Sue. She is gathering her books and is being pushed out the door by the crowd. Outside, the playground has erupted into a rambling, noisy mess of kids and balls rolling out like tumbleweeds, leaving backpacks and jackets strewn behind them. Leading one loud and rowdy group is my younger brother. He raises his hand in a wave and is carried out of sight.

After an eternity, or maybe only five minutes, we join up with our neighbor Jill. *Hurry up!* I think, but I hide my impatience and keep a snail's pace behind Sue and Jill. They are busy chatting and laughing. I half-listen while looking down at my brown and white oxfords. The rhythmic shuffle of my shoes slapping against the sidewalk transports me.

I am a jungle explorer quietly walking and listening for exotic birds and animals…

In my dream-like trance, I almost walk straight into a telephone pole.

Grabbing my cardigan, Sue pulls me sideways around the pole. "Watch where you're going!" she teases.

We continue our daily trudge up the hill. The one-block walk takes only five minutes to fly down in the mornings. But the afternoon climb can take a half hour or more. We plod our way to my house at the top of the hill. It's the first stop on our block. Sue and Jill give careless waves. They continue gossiping, sauntering up the palm-lined street. I look up to the second-floor window, seeing if I can spot my Abuelita in her little room.

Opening the heavy carved wooden front door, I catch a whiff of freshly cooked pinto beans. Running up the stairs I yell, "Abuelita, soy aquí."

Dropping my schoolbooks, sweater, and shoes in a heap at the top of the stairs, I glance around for Abuelita. *Maybe she's napping.* I dart into the bright yellow kitchen and fill a ceramic bowl from the pot bubbling on the stove. Abuelita appears from the living room.

"Solamente una pequeña siesta, Mija" she says.

My abuelita, Theodosia Mier Winstead, was born in 1884. She was ninety years old when she came to stay with us. Mom had started teaching full-time, and Abuelita came to help take care of us. I knew she was "old" and some form of a "great" grandma, but I had always just called her "Abuelita" or "Little Grandma" because at four feet nine, she was smaller than I was at age nine.

Settling myself at the breakfast counter, I blow to cool the beans.

"Una cuento, por favor, Abuelita." I look up into her lined face waiting for another one of her real-life stories.

> *One time, living in a place they call España, there was a big hotel over there where American people live and they have a parrot. That was in the state of Veracruz and there were lots of wild parrots. I want to know how a parrot taste, to see if it maybe like chicken.*
>
> *So, first time a parrot come here, I'm going get it and cook it. One day American's parrot flew to my window, I took and put him in. I told the lady who was with me, to put on a pot of water so we can cook it. I took the parrot and wring its neck. I put it in the water when I heard knock at the door.*
>
> *"Lady, lady! My poor parrot come here; did you see it? I think it flew here?" the American asks.*
>
> *"I don't know, maybe it's here someplace," I shrug and glance around. "Is this it?"*
>
> *I gesture. The poor parrot there with its neck crooked, you know, in a pot of hot water.*
>
> *"Yes—give it to me, please. Thank you very much," the American said. Then she took it, cradling its poor neck.*

So, I didn't have no parrot stew.

Abuelita laughs and shakes her head. I hop off the bar stool to hug her, then run to get another bowl of beans.

SMOKING ON BALCONY ONLY

Grandma May stomps up the stairs and gruffly asks, "Where do you want this?" as she hands off a pan of no-bake refrigerator fudge. As I give kisses, I offer to take sweaters and purses to put out of the way on Mom and Dad's bed. But Grandma May refuses to give up either. She clutches her purse to her chest as if I'm a mugger attempting to rob her blind. I shrug and run to put things in the bedroom. Then I hurry back to the kitchen, where Mom is putting the ham in the oven.

Grandma May pointedly looks at the new sign prominently displayed above the buffet, at the entrance to the kitchen. SMOKING ON BALCONY ONLY. Not that it's a new rule—Grandma has never been allowed to smoke in our house. Reading it again, she huffs and draws her sweater tighter across her chest. With a scowl, she marches to the back door and wrestles with the lock.

"Let me help!" I spryly hop over and unlatch the sliding door. With a backward dismissive wave, she's off to wander the deck with the peacocks, fervently sucking down each cigarette as if it were her last.

SEWN UP

After an afternoon of riding over the (backyard) plains, I jumped off my (picnic table) covered wagon, pulled down my bonnet, and ran into the house. My best friend Sue and I were big fans of *Little House on the Prairie* and spent many hours a day playing westward-bound pioneers.

"I need a prairie dress!" I shouted. Always the dramatic child, all my requests had a loud tone of urgency.

"Well, we can make you one," Mom calmly replied. She was seated at the white Formica table in our family room, up to her elbows in fifth-grade "How I Spent My Summer" essays.

Considering her small to-grade pile, she made a snap decision. "I can take a break, let's go!"

Bursting into a smile as wide as my face, I grabbed my butterfly tote bag. "Can I pick the fabric?" I asked.

"Sure, calico print is traditional, but let's look around when we get there," Mom replied in her typical, no-nonsense, reasonable manner.

It was a quick trip to Joann Fabric store. I picked out a McCall's Easy Stitch pattern and two tiny floral calico prints, one was tan with pink flowers and the other violet-blue. Back home, Mom set up the sewing machine with matching thread. We washed the fabric and unfolded the patterns. Then we ironed both.

"When do we start sewing?" I complained.

"Preparation is always the longest part," Mom calmly reminded me. "We need to spend the time gathering the materials, doing set-up, so that we end up with a wonderful product, just like in baking."

"I know, but it takes soooo loooooong" I whined, stretching out the last words in a painful screech as I threw myself forward onto the kitchen table.

Mom gently hushed me and lightly rubbed my back. "Take some deep breaths."

Then Mom showed me how to pin the pattern to the fabric and cut out the pieces needed for my dress. This task went quickly since the pattern only had five pieces. I was carrying things into the bedroom to start sewing when the phone rang.

"Don't answer it!" I pleaded, knowing that if Mom got on the phone, it would be at least an hour till she returned to our sewing project, she loved to chat.

She waved me off, "I'll make it quick. You have the directions right there."

I've been hand-sewing Barbie clothes with Grandma May for years—I can do this! I read the directions front to back and looked at the pictures. First, I pinned the pieces together as instructed, and then I stared down the machine and started sewing. By the time Mom got off the phone, the only step left was attaching the sleeves.

"Oh my, you've certainly been busy. You're almost done!" she exclaimed as I held up the body of the dress for her to see.

I continued to sew and even design outfits through middle and high school. In college, when I would tell anyone that I was a theatrical costumer, Mom would chime in, "I'm the one that taught Maria how to sew."

At which, I would gracefully nod and give her a kiss on her proudly flushed cheek.

HOLIDAZE

In the quiet before the storm of Christmas Eve, Jesse and I rush around the house doing last-minute prep: setting up folding tables and chairs, moving couches, and putting away scattered books. Given that we host the family every couple of months, we have the drill down. Mom is in the kitchen making the 7-Up punch and putting it in plastic jugs. She'll add the sherbet and put it out when guests arrive. "Maria, can you get the crystal punch bowl down, sweetie?" The tallest in the family, I'm always asked to retrieve items from the high kitchen cabinets.

The grandmas arrive, two by two, bearing food: Mamo and Grandma May bring fruitcake, fudge, and marshmallow treats. Grandma Mary and Abuelita arrive with the pots of steaming tamales. Then families begin arriving by the carload: kids running in one door and out the back to play, aunts pulling on aprons as they head to the kitchen, uncles hovering by the food tables.

I'm greeting everyone, grabbing coats and bags to be put on Mom's bed. Jesse is helping carry and stash the presents in the new family room. White elephant gifts in one corner, kid gifts under the tree. I can hear Dad's booming voice as he gives tours of our downstairs art gallery.

Mom is everywhere at once: organizing the food, settling my elderly great-aunts on couches, and yelling at the kids on the deck to stop chasing the peacocks. Only five feet two, Mom has a booming teacher voice and larger-than-life personality. Her generous smile and kind words make her a benevolent dictator. I shadow Mom, on hand when she needs more glass platters taken down or another chair in the living room.

The next few hours pass in blurry pandemonium as the family continues to arrive and eat in shifts. I keep busy putting out more tamales and wiping up punch spills off the shiny new hardwood floor in the family room. A space Dad constructed over the summer, it ate up my view of the backyard but opened up a rectangular space with windows on three sides, perfect for entertaining. At the peak of the night, we have over one hundred relatives in the house.

Grandma Mary has given permission for presents to be opened before midnight. We gather the younger cousins around the tree and pass out their gifts. After the flurry of squeals and shredding wrapping paper dissipates, Mom directs the little kids to the living room to watch holiday movies. Jesse and I set up the chairs in a large circle for the white elephant gifting. All my cousins steal and fight over a couple of brightly wrapped packages with gold bows that Aunt Ruth brought.

Abuelita magically pulls out grocery bags with small wrapped packages for all of her great-great-grandchildren. She has spent months crocheting slippers for each one of us. Putting them on, we take turns sliding up and down the polished hardwood floor, laughing as we collapse in heaps, like bowling pins, at the end of the room.

In the early morning hours, after an endless stream of hugs and good-bye kisses, a warm silence descends on the house. Jesse and I run around picking up wrapping paper, bows, and discarded plates and cups. Jesse sweeps while I mop. Mom hand-washes the glass platters and punch bowl while Dad dries.

I squint and look at the clock, only six hours till Mamo and Grandma May return for Christmas morning breakfast and Santa presents. I shuffle off to bed to dream of the day ahead.

PAN DULCE

When I was in middle school, we had a professional art gallery on the first floor of my house. Dad and my uncles would rotate their paintings every couple of months. Sometimes they would host other guest artists. On Saturdays when there was a new show opening, we would wake up early. My brother, Jesse, and I would run around tidying the house. Dad went to the local panderia to pick up the pan dulce and Mexican hot chocolate. I loved its thick, bitter, slightly spicy-sweet taste.

The upstairs, including our bedrooms, had to be visitor ready—nothing left out, no clothes strewn about on the floor or back of chairs, no shoes hiding under the coffee table or couches. Our walls were covered in framed paintings and drawings from the carpet to the support beams of the fifteen-foot ceilings. Visitors might ask to see additional works and be shown upstairs at any time.

In preparation for the gallery opening, I would curl my long dark hair and put on lip gloss. I liked wearing my sixth-grade graduation dress or one of the prairie dresses I had sewn myself. After stealing a peek in Mom's full-length mirror, I rushed downstairs to set up.

I was in charge of the guestbook and refreshing the sweets table. I lined up the pan dulce by colors: pink, yellow, and white. The pig cookies to the right and empanadas to the left. Once the napkins were fanned out and the cups were stacked in small piles of six, I situated myself at the entry table. I would greet each guest and ask them to sign in. Then, with a Vanna White–like sweep of my arm, I would direct them to enter the gallery to my left so that they looped back to the sweets, instead of starting there and spreading crumbs throughout the house.

Since I looked much older than my thirteen years, I often received unwanted attention. Marveling at my height and long tan limbs, patrons asserted, "You should be a model!"

Peering out from under my feathered Farrah-style locks, I cringed and blushed. Uncle Jude boomed out, "Of course, she's modeled, her dad's an artist. There are drawings of her everywhere."

PAINTED

Bright, bouncing babe
rolling, crawling, tumbling
across the sketchbook page
study of toddler eating
with broad toothy grins

Busy preschooler captured in bright colors
running, skipping, leaping
off the page and onto bold murals
round doll-like face with
wide green eyes looking out

Pre-teen years
placed in hard-to-hold poses
till limbs and thoughts grow numb
on display in photos and paintings
desperate to break the glass
and fly free

GRANDMA MARY'S EMPANADA RECIPE

Ingredients:

Filling
1 can of crushed pineapple (drain juice)
1 cup brown sugar

Dough
2 cups all-purpose flour
2 tablespoons white cane sugar
1 teaspoon baking powder
1 teaspoon salt
¾ cup shortening
½ cup of water

Instructions:

Preheat oven to 350°F. In a small saucepan, combine filling ingredients and heat on medium.

While filling ingredients heat, in a large bowl, mix the dry ingredients. Add in the shortening and water as needed to moisten, until the dough clings to itself. Divide dough into 1-inch balls and roll out ovals on a floured surface to about a quarter-inch even thickness. Lay the oblong piece of dough vertically on a baking sheet. Place a generous tablespoon of filling in the center. Fold the dough in half and finger pinch the edges together to form a scalloped semi-circle. Repeat with each piece of dough. Bake for 30 minutes. Makes about a dozen empanadas.

PHONE CALL

Even though I lived in a different state, Mom was always just a phone call away. We talked at least once a day, usually around dinnertime. With two young daughters and a part-time job, I was always scrambling with what to cook for dinner. Adding to my struggle was the fact that Riley was on a gluten-free diet, and Mac was on a white-food diet of pasta and cheese.

The phone is ringing as I open the door.

"Hi Mom," I exclaim, dropping my bag on the counter. "Yup, just walked in. Hold on." Turning back to the girls, I remind them to hang up their coats. "Help," I continue, hopelessly rummaging through the fridge. "I can't make pasta again."

"Kids weren't such picky eaters when you were young," Mom says. "Even though Jesse basically lived on white bread peanut butter sandwiches."

"As if I could even give my kids PB&J sandwiches," I lament and stare blankly at the fridge shelves.

"They sure didn't have all these crazy food allergies," Mom observes.

"I know, snacks for Mac's pre-school class are just rice crackers and water." I pull out some cheese sticks for the girls. "As a kid, I ate everything," I declare.

"Except the pig's feet," Mom laughs.

"Oh, that was the worst!" I cry. "What were you thinking?"

"Mamo used to make it for me as a treat when I was a child." Mom's voice dips a little. "You were so stubborn," she recalls. "You sat there for hours and refused to eat it."

"Yup, wasn't going to touch a pig foot," I laugh. "That quivering gelatinous mass was horrifying!"

"Well, I never cooked that again." She pauses and suggests, "Hmmm, what about a casserole? The girls love my enchiladas."

"Yes! I've got cheese and corn tortillas!" I call out, "Girls, say bye," and hold up the phone.

Their sweet voices sing out, "Love you, Nana!" as I hang up.

LEMON MERINGUE PIE

"First, cut in the softened butter," Mom instructs. She is teaching Riley, my oldest daughter at age six, how to make her signature dessert. Riley takes a blunt butter knife and slowly starts to blend it into the flour. Mac, my youngest, happily watches from her highchair, stacks of Cheerios piled upon her tray. I'm the sous-chef, pulling ingredients, washing bowls and measuring cups. Baking is not a skill of mine, so I'm pleased that Mom is the one doing the teaching.

After rolling the dough, Mom puts the pie crust in the oven. "While the crust is baking, we start the custard." Mom shows Riley how to grate and juice the lemons. "You need the juice from three lemons and the grated rind from at least one. Your papa likes his pie nice and tart," she chuckles.

"*Pie!*" Mac calls out from the highchair, wanting to be included.

"Yes, in a little bit, after it cools." She drops a kiss on the top of Mac's sweaty brow. The small kitchen is warm with the oven on, and Mac has always run hot.

"Stir the custard slowly in a figure eight." Always the teacher, Mom gently guides Riley's hand as she stirs the custard. Focused on the task, Riley teeters on her tiny step stool and I reach out to steady her, but my mom is there with her arm on Riley's back. Intent on the thickening custard, Riley doesn't even notice the wobble.

"Now we beat the eggs for the meringue till it stands up in peaks," Mom calmly instructs as she assembles the electric beater. Riley has moved her stool over and stands poised by the counter. "It's important to keep it low in the bowl so that you don't splatter egg everywhere. If your arms get tired, let me or your mom know, and we can help."

But Riley has that determined look on her face, and I know that even if her arms are drooping with fatigue, she won't ask for help. I stay on the periphery, doing kitchen clean up and keeping Mac quiet with snacks. I'm grateful for this precious time with my mom, baking up memories.

ICE CREAM FOR BREAKFAST

After the late flight, hospital check-out, and downtown traffic, I don't set a morning alarm. My mom and I wake to the sun streaming in from the east-facing windows.

Always a chipper person, she exclaims, "The light is lovely in this room!" She leaps up and runs to the closet. Mom handles and rejoices over each item as if brand new, commenting on the colors and fabric textures. She picks up a sweater and pets it as she continues to prattle on about everything and nothing at all.

After a fashion show of brightly printed blouses, Mom twirls and we head to the kitchen. She plops herself at the breakfast counter, her feet dangling and swinging back and forth as she continues her relentless chatter. Meanwhile, I search the cupboards for anything resembling coffee. Suddenly there is a break in the stream of words, and she brightly asks, "Can I have ice cream?"

I pause in my digging through the pantry. I'm shocked: my practical, no frills, no-dessert-till-you've-eaten-your-broccoli mother now has a bottomless sweets craving.

Mentally reviewing the short information sheet the hospital gave me, I recall two details.

Patient needs lots of rest and a consistent schedule.
Provide healthy options at mealtimes.

Frozen yogurt is a sweet dairy product, I rationalize. *Why not?* Anyone would want a treat after a month of eating only hospital food. I open the freezer and find her favorite flavor, French Vanilla, in the back of the freezer along with some coffee beans.

There is a lull in her verbal ramblings as she slowly eats her frozen yogurt one small spoonful at a time. I listen to the drip of the percolator and breathe in the rich, warm aroma.

"Mamo drank coffee every morning," Mom reminds me. "But I don't like the taste of it, only the smell." She laughs and sticks out her tongue at me, leaving me feeling like the mom of a silly teen. I pour my coffee into a to-go mug and gather the paperwork for our errands.

Driving us around town in her brand-new red diesel VW Jetta, I suddenly find myself lost. I pull over to input the directions into the GPS. But surprisingly, she has already input the address for the bank, so off we go. The sharp and proper English-accented voice grates on as I drive down Western Ave. The GPS keeps commanding me to make a U-turn before—

Recalculating…
Recalculating…
Recalculating…

I return to using the shortcuts from when I lived here thirty years ago. The GPS keeps insisting on U-turns and recalculating until I want to scream and throw it out the window.

Mom pauses in her chirping commentary. "It's just a machine," she chuckles. She reaches over and turns it off.

Parking at the bank, I instruct her to "only answer direct questions and sit quietly, please."

I have all the necessary forms to be added to the accounts and can't let on that Mom had a stroke. When asked, Mom can recall every account number and her social security number with no hesitation. Back in the car, she beams as if she has just won a gold ribbon.

"Can we stop for a cookie?" she begs.

"After we have some protein," I remind her, as I would with my two young daughters.

We settle into a table at the local coffee shop. As we wait for our lunch order, she drops her endless bright chatter.

She leans forward and in a hushed, secretive voice says, "Remember to get an account and credit card in your name. For emergencies."

Then, like the sun coming out from behind a cloud, she's back to rambling about her fellow teachers. She's stuck in the past as if she was at school teaching yesterday, even though she's been retired two years now.

After she finishes her sandwich, I hand over a large chocolate chip cookie, her favorite. Mom smiles with delight and starts breaking off small pieces, savoring them a bite at a time.

FIFTEEN THINGS I MISS ABOUT MY MOM

1. Her full wide-tooth grin that lit up a room.

2. Her happy chatter about the girls, weather, and food.

3. Her physical touch—hugs, pats, stroking my hair, showed me how much she cared.

4. Her phone calls—asking questions about my friends and their kids, always interested and invested in my life.

5. Her laugh and positive outlook, how grateful she was for everything.

6. Her constant support, acknowledgment, and encouragement of me as a working parent trying to balance it all.

7. Sharing books. We were both fast and avid readers, we could read a book or more daily, and loved chatting about them.

8. Crying over emotional scenes in rom coms, keeping a tissue box between us.

9. Going out shopping together and her wanting to get the same coat or sweater or boots that I had, such a wonderful compliment looking back at it now.

10. Playing games: my mom was a great speller and had a quick wit. She loved playing cards and board games, especially Scrabble.

11. Her hugs always made me feel better when I was sad or low.

12. Her off-key singing voice while she sang along to songs on the radio.

13. The sweet nicknames for me and my girls: pumpkin pie, angel pie, and sweetie.

14. The sparkle in her bright green eyes when she looked at me.

15. The first tangy bite of her lemon meringue pie, with its perfect peaks and caramelized marshmallows on top.

LEMON MERINGUE PIE RECIPE

Ingredients:

½ cup cold water
7 tablespoons cornstarch
3 eggs
1½ cups hot water
1¼ cups sugar
3 lemons (grated rind and juice)
1 tablespoon butter or margarine
1 prebaked pie shell

Instructions:

Mix cold water and cornstarch to a thin paste. Separate egg yolks and whites. Put whites in the refrigerator, and beat the yolks in a bowl. Combine hot water and sugar in a saucepan and bring to a boil over high heat. Add cornstarch paste, and cook until mixture begins to thicken, stirring constantly. Once the thick mixture boils, reduce heat to medium. Stir a small amount of the hot mixture into yolks to warm, then add yolks into the saucepan, stirring well.

Add lemon rind and juice. Add butter and combine well. Remove from heat, stirring occasionally, and pour into the pie shell once the mixture is at room temperature.

Meringue topping:

>3 egg whites
>4 tablespoons sugar
>1 teaspoon vanilla extract
>10 mini marshmallows

Instructions:

Heat oven to 325°F. Beat egg whites with an electric beater on high until they hold a stiff peak. Add sugar 1 tablespoon at a time, then add vanilla, beating continuously. Pile meringue lightly on pie, do not spread around too much or it will lose shape. Place mini marshmallows in a spiral pattern on top. Bake 25 to 30 minutes until meringue is lightly browned.

EPILOGUE: THE STORYTELLER

I tried holding the memories
deep inside and cocooned—
till they burst
like butterflies
swarming the sky.

Monarchs and matriarchs
brilliant yellows and blues
glittering in the sun
shining forth
for you—my little one.

I dream of the future
a wise grandma I'll be
with you settled on my knee
eyes looking up
as the stories pour forth.

For I carry all our ancestors
nested inside of me—
my writing provides a voice,
take and sing our tales—
as a way to carry on.

AUTHOR'S NOTES

I: La Cocina

As a young widow, Abuelita worked in the cannery and lived with her granddaughter Mary and her family. Abuelita rotated houses and spent time in El Paso with her daughter-in-law Manuela. But in my childhood memories, she was always there at Grandma Mary's house.

Matriarchal Ode

Even though both my parents spoke Spanish and my mom was a bilingual teacher, I only learned Spanish in middle school.

Christmas Eve Tamales

As a child, I assumed that Abuelita, the matriarch, was the person who held all the family recipes and traditions. Only recently, I discovered that Abuelita learned to cook tamales while in her forties from her daughter-in-law, Manuela.

Questions for Manuela de Jesus

Much like secret ingredients and lost recipes, many of the histories of women in our family are hidden. Great-Grandma Manuela died on the farm in Ensenada, Baja California, Mexico, while Mom was pregnant with me. Manuela's story was buried with her. My questions grew out of ancestral research.

II: Southern Hospitality

Great-Grandma Mamo and Grandma May had a contentious mother-daughter relationship. They were always bickering and arguing, but also were each other's only support for most of their lives. They were both widowed young in their forties. They had dinner together every night and coffee together each morning. It made financial sense for them to live together after my youngest aunt got married.

Cast Iron

My research shows that Mamo was at least a quarter Cherokee Indian, but she denied that part of her heritage and never spoke of it.

Baking Memories

After going through the entire recipe box, the only item I found written in Mamo's handwriting was a cleaning solution for removing tough stains.

III: Home Sweet Home

My great-great-grandfather Frank Winstead; his son, James Winstead; and baby Winstead are all buried in the local San Pedro Cemetery, which was next to the small one-bedroom house where both my Dad and I spent our early childhood.

Pies

As part of my ancestral research, I received a box of cassette tapes that my aunts had saved. Included was a tape of Mom telling stories to some of my younger cousins.

Yellow

In 1972, when I was six years old, we moved out of the Denison house and into a new three-thousand-square-foot house that Dad designed and built.

Smoking on Balcony Only

A neighbor bought a pair of peacocks and let them roam wild. Now there is a huge band of wild peacocks in the neighborhood. There are no predators so they just keep breeding and multiplying.

Holidaze

I wonder if Mom realized that she would be hosting every family event for the next twenty years when Dad showed her the design for the new San Pedro house.

ACKNOWLEDGMENTS

Everything I write is a love letter to my mom. She encouraged and always believed in me. She created a wonderful safe space in which I could explore, learn, and grow during my childhood. She and my grandmothers were always generous with their time and attention. I am grateful for their unconditional love and support.

Many thanks to my daughters for being my first audience. Your belief in and feedback on my work has kept me writing. We have always been storytellers and will continue to be.

I want to thank and acknowledge my two aunts who have researched and saved our family documents. I'm appreciative of all you have shared with me. My writing is richer and deeper because of the histories that you shared.

Maria Gutierrez was raised in Southern California as part of a large Mexican American family. She received her BA from Pomona College and her MPA from The Evans School at the University of Washington. Maria currently lives in Seattle with her husband and her dog. Her two grown daughters are away at college. She enjoys reading, taking long neighborhood walks, and cooking family recipes.

maria-gutierrez.com